Disgusting Body Facts

Ooze and Goo

Angela Royston

Raintree

Chicago, Illinois

www.heinemannraintree.com
Visit our website to find out
more information about
Heinemann-Raintree books.

To order:
☎ Phone 888-454-2279
▣ Visit www.heinemannraintree.com
to browse our catalog and order online.

Edited by Nancy Dickmann, Sian Smith, and
  Rebecca Rissman
Designed by Joanna Hinton Malivoire
Original illustrations ©Capstone Global Library 2010
Original illustrations by Christian Slade
Picture research by Tracy Cummins and Tracey Engel
Originated by Capstone Global Library Ltd
Printed and bound in China by Leo Paper Products Ltd

14 13 12 11 10
10 9 8 7 6 5 4 3 2 1

**Library of Congress Cataloging-in-Publication
Data**
Royston, Angela.
  Ooze and goo / Angela Royston.
    p. cm. -- (Disgusting body facts)
  Includes bibliographical references and index.
  ISBN 978-1-4109-3746-9 (hc)
  ISBN 978-1-4109-3752-0 (pb)
1. Body fluids--Juvenile literature. 2. Human body-
-Juvenile literature. 3. Human physiology--Juvenile
literature. I. Title.
  QP90.5.R69 2010
  612'.01522--dc22
                          2009022243

Acknowledgments
The author and publisher are grateful to the following
for permission to reproduce copyright material:
Alamy pp. **6** (©David Crausby), **22** (©Medical-on-
Line); Getty Images pp. **13** (©The Image Bank/David
Trood), **26** (©Seymour Hewitt), **27** (©Stone/Andy
Roberts); istockphoto p. **29** (©Holly Sisson); Photo
Researchers, Inc. pp. **11 top** (©Scimat), **17** (©Dr. P.
Marazzi), **21** (©Edward Kinsman); Photolibrary p. **25**
(©Blend Images); Phototake p. **15** (©Pulse Picture
Library/CMP Images); Shutterstock pp. **9** (©Graca
Victoria) **11 bottom** (©Oberon); Visuals Unlimited,
Inc. p. **19** (©Ralph Hutchings).

Cover photograph of a woman's tongue dripping
saliva reproduced with permission of Getty Images
(©David Trood).

Every effort has been made to contact copyright
holders of material reproduced in this book. Any
omissions will be rectified in subsequent printings if
notice is given to the publisher.

All the Internet addresses (URLs) given in this book
were valid at the time of going to press. However, due
to the dynamic nature of the Internet, some addresses
may have changed, or sites may have changed or
ceased to exist since publication. While the author and
publisher regret any inconvenience this may cause
readers, no responsibility for any such changes can be
accepted by either the author or the publisher.

Some words are shown in bold, **like this**. You can find
out what they mean by looking in the glossary.

Contents

Slimy Insides

The inside of your body is slimy and slippery. A liquid called **mucus** lines many tubes in your body. Sometimes mucus leaks out as snot and spit.

Did You Know?

Mucus is not the only thing that leaks from your body. Other things include **earwax**, blood, and **pus**.

snot

earwax

spit

pus

5

Snot

Snot is **mucus** in your nose. Snot helps to trap dirt and **germs** that you breathe in. Germs can make you sick. When you have a cold, your nose makes lots of extra mucus. The mucus washes out some of the germs.

6

booger

Did You Know?

A booger is dried snot in your nose. Some people pick their noses to remove a booger! Other people just blow their noses.

Coughing up Mucus

The tubes that join your mouth and nose to your **lungs** are lined with **mucus**, too. When you are sick, the mucus becomes thick and sticky. Then you cough to clear the tubes.

phlegm

When you cough, the mucus comes into your mouth. It is called **phlegm** (say "flem"). Mucus contains **germs**, so never touch someone else's snot or phlegm.

Why Is Phlegm Sometimes Green?

When you are sick, your **phlegm** might be yellow or green. Your body makes chemicals to kill **germs** when you are sick. The iron in the chemicals turns your phlegm green.

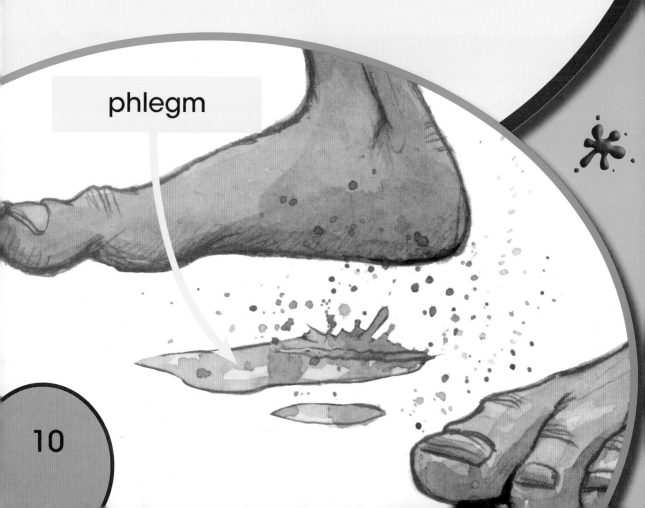

phlegm

microscope

These are germs seen through a microscope.

Did You Know?

Germs are too small to see without a microscope. It could take a million of them to cover the head of a pin.

Saliva and Spit

Your mouth makes **saliva**, or spit, all the time. When you are asleep, saliva sometimes dribbles out of your mouth. It makes your pillow wet!

Did You Know?

Some people spit when they speak. As they talk, a shower of spit sprays into the air!

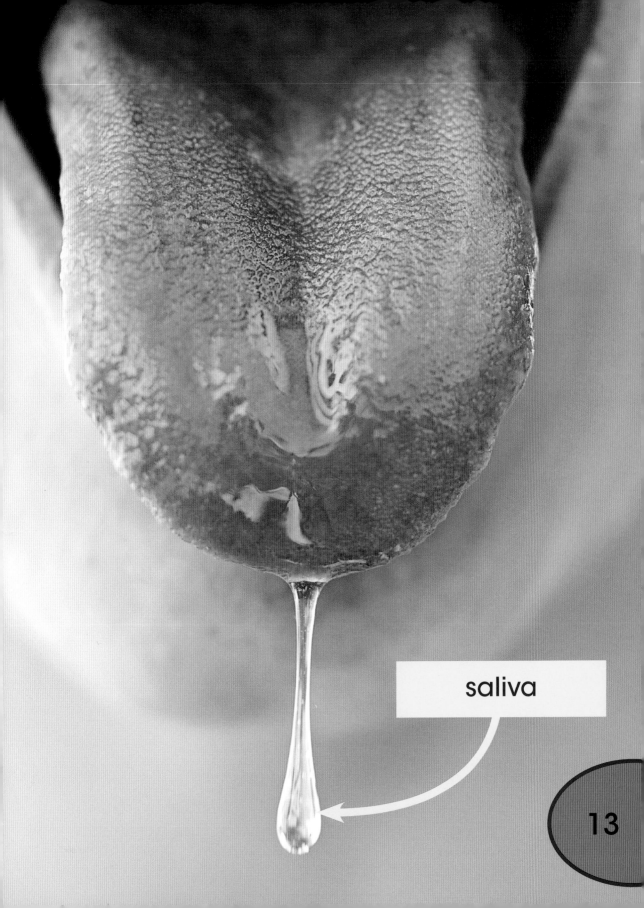

saliva

13

Earwax

Earwax keeps your ears clean! Wax slowly makes its way out of your ears. Any dirt comes out with it. Sometimes the wax sticks together to make an orange-yellow lump.

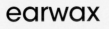

earwax

This photo shows a buildup of earwax. Having lots of earwax in your ear can make it hard to hear.

Conjunctivitis

Pinkeye gives you sticky goo on your eyelids. The goo makes it hard to open your eyes in the morning. Pinkeye is also called **conjunctivitis**. It is caused by a type of **germ** called **bacteria**.

conjunctivitis

Did You Know?

Sometimes goo collects in the corners of your eyes while you are asleep. This is different from conjunctivitis. It is easy to wipe this goo away.

Bleeding

If you get a scrape or small cut on your skin, blood oozes out. Don't panic! Bleeding washes out dirt and **germs**. You still need to clean the cut or scrape under running water. Then cover it with a bandage.

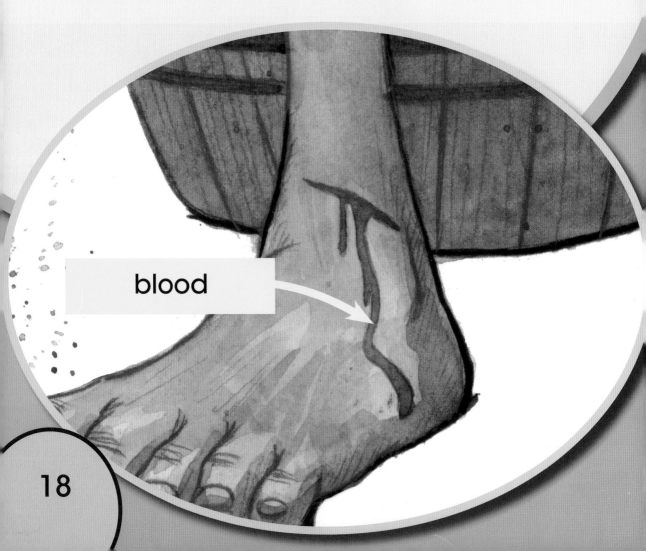

blood

narrow tubes called blood vessels

Tiny, narrow tubes carry blood through your skin. Each tube is narrower than a hair on your head.

WARNING
If you cut yourself, find someone to help you.

Scabs

A small cut or scrape will stop bleeding after a short time. This is because the blood in the cut or scrape becomes thicker. It forms a thick blob. This thick blob slowly dries to form a hard scab.

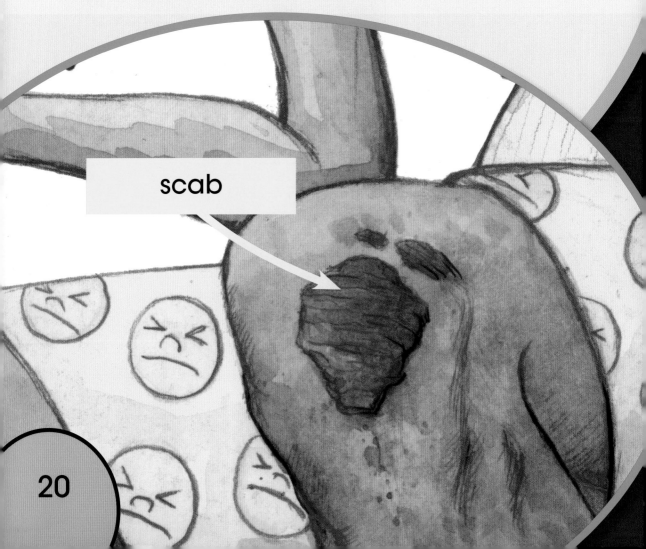

scab

scab

new skin

> ### ! WARNING
> Don't pick a scab! It may make the cut bleed again. New skin grows below the scab. The scab falls off, bit by bit.

Boils

A boil is a sore that is filled with **pus** the boil bursts, the pus oozes out. Pus is a thick liquid. It contains **germs** from inside the sore.

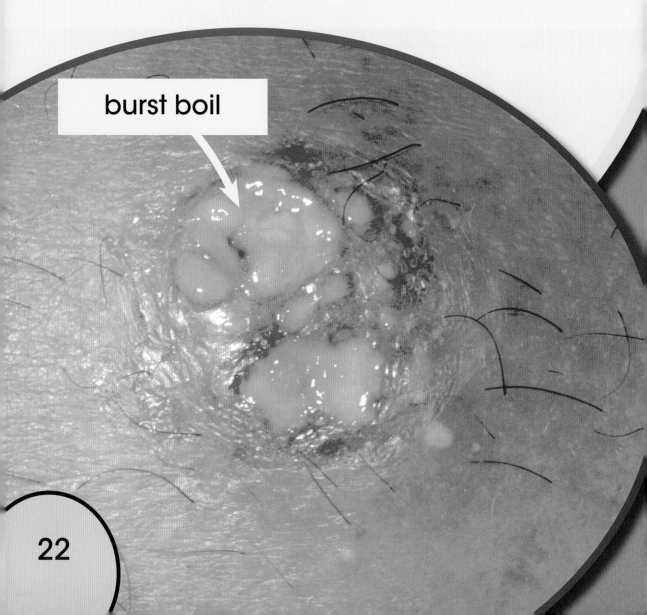

burst boil

pus

FUN FACT
Pus is usually white or yellow. It can be green, brown, or even blue!

23

Sweat

Sweat is liquid that oozes out of your skin. Sweat helps to keep you cool. The hotter you are, the more you sweat. Old sweat may become smelly.

Sweat under armpits can be really smelly!

Did You Know?

Running around makes you sweat even more. Soccer players can lose 2.5 gallons of sweat a day. That's the same as about 36 glasses of water.

25

Smelly Feet

Your feet sweat. They sweat even more when you wear sneakers. Old sweat in your sneakers makes your sneakers stink, too.

Did You Know?

Toe jam is the dirt that can collect between your toes. It is a mixture of sweat, dead skin, and fluff from your socks.

toe jam

More About Body Fluids

More than half of your body is water.

Blood and pee are mostly water. So are **saliva**, **mucus**, snot, and tears.

You lose more than 35 ounces of water every day. You lose most of it in pee, sweat, poo, and in the air you breathe out.

You should drink about 35 to 70 ounces of liquid a day. This will help to replace the water you lose.

You make about 35 to 70 ounces of saliva every day.

35 to 70 ounces is about 4 to 8 glasses.

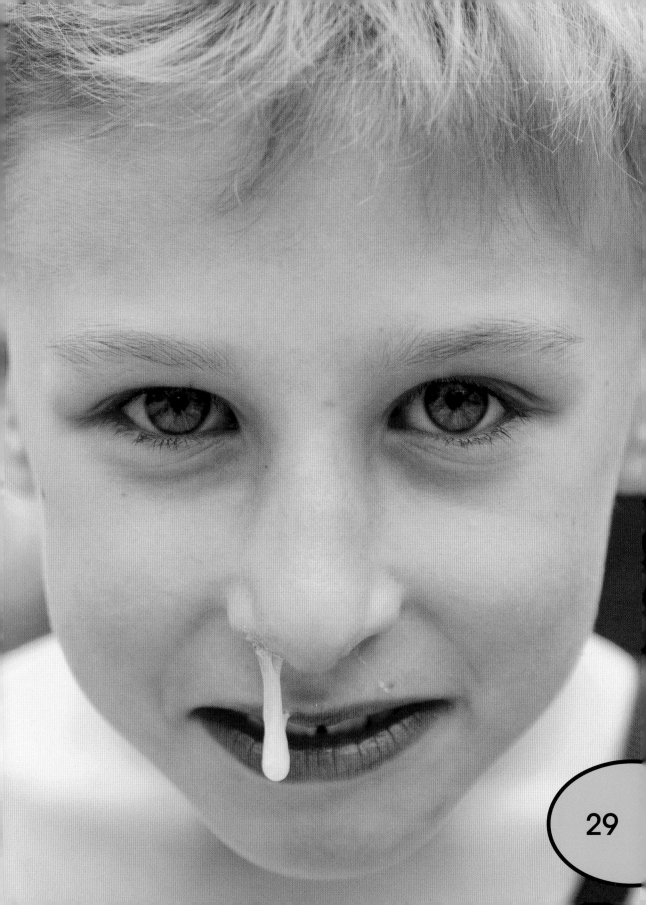

Glossary

bacteria tiny living things. Bacteria are a type of germ.

conjunctivitis illness that affects the inside of the eyelid

earwax soft, yellow wax that is made by the skin in the ear

germ tiny living thing that can make you sick if it gets inside your body

lungs parts of your body where air goes when you breathe in. You have two lungs in your chest.

mucus slimy liquid that lines the tubes inside your body

phlegm mucus made in your breathing tubes

pus thick yellow or white liquid that forms when a cut is infected by germs

saliva liquid made in the mouths of people, insects, and other kinds of animals. Saliva is also called "spit."

Find Out More

Find out

How do you catch pinkeye?

Books

Barnhill, Kelly Regan. *The Amazingly Gross Human Body: The Sweaty Book of Sweat.* Mankato, MN: Capstone, 2009.

Royston, Angela. *How's Your Health? Colds, the Flu, and Other Infections*. Mankato, MN: Smart Apple Media, 2009.

Taylor, Barbara. *The Best Book of the Human Body*. New York: Kingfisher, 2008.

Websites

http://kidshealth.org/kid/ill_injure/sick/colds.html
This Website tells you about colds and mucus. It also explains how your body fights germs.

http://kidshealth.org/kid/ill_injure/sick/conjunctivitis.html
This Website provides facts about pinkeye.

www.thechildrenshospital.org/wellness/info/kids/22392.aspx
This Website tells you all about boogers.

Index